Copyright

Title book: My Love Story
Author book: Choying Huynh

© 2022, Choying Huynh/Integration Meditation, LLC
Self publishing
integrationmeditation@gmail.com

Love Story

Discovering my own love story by walking
from warrior to hero's journey.

We each have a love story, many times over
in our life. Our love stories seem to be never
ending, no matter how many times we are
broken or experience breakups. There is one
Love Story that many seem to overlook; the
relationship we have with ourselves.
Our journey in life through our reflections,
healing, connections, dreams, passion and
purpose.
Our soul yearns for us to awaken...

To remember ourselves and who we truly
are...
This is our very own love story.

With loving gratitude...

I dedicate this to all life, nature, souls, friends and family past, present and future. Especially those who gave their time and loving energy into this book. They helped and supported me in making this book what it is today. I give each of them special gratitude and words of kindness which can be found at the back of the book. I also dedicate this to all my students and people I came across in my studio spaces. Amazing learning and growth over the last few years, for all of us because of our paths crossing.

You are all Love, Powerful and Sovereign!

My Beautiful Daughters
His Eminence Shyalpa Tenzin Rinpoche
Caitlin Leigh Fluegge
Emerald Raye
Holly Finnegan
Joseph Williams
Shashwat Bhardwaj
Yannae Kemp
Yvette Van Dam

Kind words of Love and Encouragement

"I commend Choying Huynh for his work in documenting his path toward spiritual awakening. He writes of the challenges, obstacles, insights and rewards, the learning and unlearning, that he has experienced on his journey toward self-mastery. Now he genuinely seeks to share his experience with others so that they too can find true purpose and meaning in their precious human lives."

---His Eminence Shyalpa Tenzin Rinpoche

"Choying has a profound way of guiding you back to your inner light by embracing the shadow. He shares beautiful and empowering tools that will help you navigate life, bringing you back to your inner light. He is a teacher who has walked the journey himself, and continues to selflessly guide others to do the same. Thank you for sharing your light, and helping us remember the truth of who we are. Empowering read!"

---Caitlin Leigh Fluegge

"This book was so insightful and inspiring. While this book is easy to read, it somehow took me on an internal journey of self discovery that I've yet to experience with other amazing " self awareness" books. I highly recommend this book if you are looking to find/connect with your inner treasures. I'm extremely thankful to Choying Huynh for sharing his story. I feel it was written with transparency, grace and love. A true gem!"

---*Emerald Raye of Light*

"Choying's journey, as he outlines in this book, depicts the many struggles he's gone through and how his own self-discovery has led him to break free from these struggles and heal. Choying whole-heartedly gives life his all, is a true observer of his own life and applies what he's learned back into himself. With his true passion for wanting to help people who want to help themselves, he guides you through how to understand your own struggles from your own perspective - but you have to be committed and do "the work".

---*Holly Finnegan*

"I first met Choying in Nepal during Kopan's month-long annual Lam Rim retreat. During the first meeting itself, Choying came off as one of the friendliest people had met during the retreat and made a friendship that lasts to this day. We immediately built a great rapport and a formidable bond. We had many great discussions and excursions during our month-long sojourn.

One of the best highlights during the town was that under the initiative Choying we created a group to learn and share our teachings related to the physical body, especially martial arts. There was a Motley Crew of young travelers everybody bring something new to the table from Yoga, healing, MMA, etc. Which was an otherwise boring and dull retreat Choying made it interesting by bringing in elements of physical workout and training at a place which didn't encourage too much exercise and let alone touching or even talking since it was a silent retreat.

(more)..

Cont'd

One of my biggest surprises was that Choying looked surprisingly young for his age. As I got to know him more I learned that he was well trained in Wing Chun.

I had always wanted to learn martial arts and I am glad my first experience came under the guidance of Choying. He taught me about the very interesting history of martial arts which arises in my own country and I didn't even know it. He went on to teach me about the evolution of martial arts to its present form today and some basics which seem practical to me as of this writing.Another aspect of friendship with Choying is that he is very passionate about inner work and the most beautiful part is that he makes it a very collective practice which otherwise is very individualistic for those who are into it. While practicing, he helps us confront our emotions which we are otherwise suppressing in our psyches.

(more)..

Cont'd

His teachings are focused on sovereignty, integrity, and making us whole as individuals. One of the best qualities of Choying is, his amazing sense of humor which even the greatest masters forget in their journey. Among his other great qualities are that he is a great friend, teacher, Shaman, and most importantly an amazing human being. He is the most humble, grounded, compassionate, and authentic person I have met. He is a great martial artist, Shaman, and now a writer."

I could go on and on about writing about the well-rounded personality of Choying, but without further ado, I will ask you to find out about his practice straight from the horse's mouth, the man himself. Before you get started here's one last thing I would like to tell you is that Choying practices what he preaches so brace yourself for an adventure."

---Shashwat. With Love. From India.

"This is a tool for the soul to find its way. Choying has been able to offer humanity love in word form. We live in a world that is focused on disconnecting our souls from our human experience. The disconnect is so great that we fall further and further from our souls intention. This in many ways is the fall of man. This journey is a journey of rediscovering our divinity and source provides the conduits that allow source to teach us how to navigate this human experience. The way this book is delivered will provide anyone, no matter the level of spiritual understandingthey are in with clarity on how to allow their soul to lead. In the most loving way Choying points us to our depths, and takes us on the soul's journey. Each chapter provides a window in to his path, while assisting us in understanding how to peel back the layers of this worlds suffering so our soul can emerge, and we can operate in the highest vibration of love. Thank you Choying, for being Love, showing love, and giving us a timeless gift."

---Yannae Kemp

"Not being gifted with a talent for languages, Choying shows just with the existence of this book the true warrior he is. He shows there are no limits when it comes to what you are capable of, just the ones we believe in ourselves. Even better, in this book, he guides us through his experiences and tools to actually move past our own conditioning. So that, not only he, but also the reader can move past his or her self-believed limitations. For me, having read it up to four times already, the book keeps showing me new things, raises new questions and keeps me exploring. That is, to me, exactly the strength of this book. Therefore, I would definitely invite you to do the same. Read it. Contemplate, and decide and experience for yourself what is true for you!"

---Yvette Van Dam

"First of all it's an honor to know you and be your friend.
I finished your book and it is amazing.
I resonate with the entire book , but here are a few
things that I love. "I operate my life knowing my
conscious, subconscious mind, boundaries ,attachments,
detachments, desires, wants and creations .The longer
you sit the more space you create.We are conditioned
young age with something as simple of choosing ice
cream."

---Joseph Willams

Table of Contents

Timeline

Dedications with love and gratitude.

Intention

The idea and outline for this book started when I began to map out my own experiences in a timeline format. In doing so, I discovered and learned to understand some of my own major synchronicities, behavior patterns and thought patterns.

The thing is, nothing in life is a coincidence or an accident. Everything in us is imprinted and created before we are even born. Whether you agree or disagree, this is not up for debate, or an opinion, or a form of education.

This is my personal experience! Living my own spiritual experiences and based on my own knowledge gained through meditation. All of this has helped me discover the true nature of who I am.

I was able to map out this process in a follow along format that I now want to share with you to help you navigate and journey through your own life events and write your own love story.

This book is meant as a workbook for you to navigate and understand your own life experiences and inner landscape. You can use it either as a stand alone guide or as a supporting guide to my 'Navigating the Mind' workshop. Either way, you will learn how to gain access to your own inner wisdom and power which is something we all have.

I start by sharing my timeline with you. What I did, what I learned and some of my experiences. Then I go into detail describing the steps in my process that had the biggest impacted on my awakening.

As you work your own way through this book, you'll be mapping out your own patterns, thoughts and major life events that have created the "you" that you are today. Create your own path of stepping into the unknown - into your own hero's journey. And map out your most important love story - your relationship with yourself.

My Timeline Summary

This timeline shows the most significant events in my life which have deepened my journey of self-discovery.

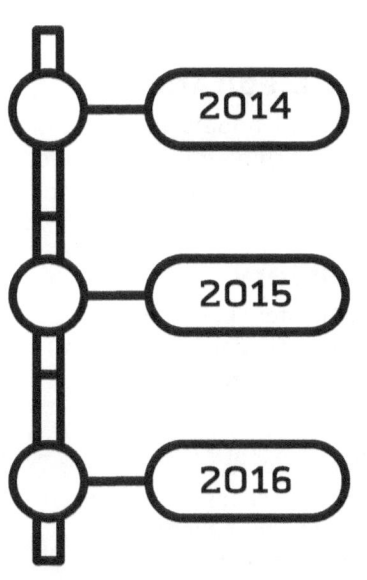

2014

Awakening

I awoke, in my Dream State, filled with love and compassion, feeling connected to everything and everyone on this planet. It was an experience of enlightenment and oneness.

2015

Costa Rica & Peru

I quit my 9-5 job with no backup plans. Then I went to Costa Rica for a 21 day fasting retreat and Peru for an ayahuasca healing retreat.

2016

Nepal & Trekking

I journeyed to Nepal to experience meditation in the Buddhist Monastery, and trekked for 5 days to the mountain.

My Timeline Summary

This timeline shows the most significant events in my life which have deepened my journey of self-discovery.

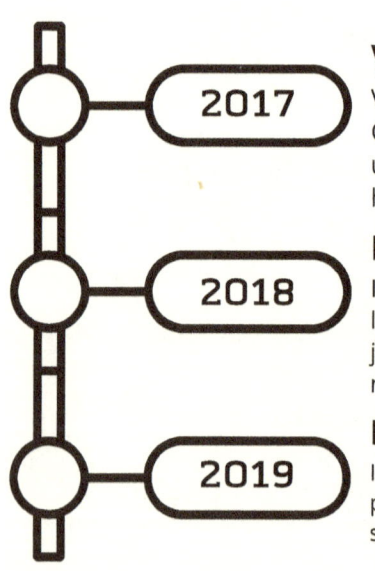

Volunteer & Meditation
Volunteered at Tara Mandala, in Colorado. Began teaching meditation and understanding the mind when I returned home.

Nepal Monastery
I revisited the Monastery in Nepal for a longer retreat. Dove deeper into my own journey of the Buddha 's teachings and meditation.

Integration
I began facilitating workshops, meditation programs, and 72 transformations at the studio. Integrating mind and body as one.

Timeline Details

2014
Awakening

I awoke, in my Dream State, filled with love and compassion, feeling connected to everything and everyone on this planet. It was an experience of enlightenment and oneness.

Timeline Details

2015
Costa Rica & Peru

I quit my 9-5 job with no backup plans. Then I went to Costa Rica for a 21 day fasting retreat and Peru for an ayahuasca healing retreat.

Timeline Details

2016
Nepal

I took a trip to Nepal to meditate in the Buddhist Monastery and trekked for 5 days to the mountain.

Timeline Details

2017
Volunteer & Meditation

Volunteered at Tara Mandala, in Colorado.
Began teaching meditation and understanding the mind
when I returned home.

Timeline Details

2018
Nepal Second Time

I revisited the Monastery in Nepal for a longer retreat.
Dove deeper into my own journey of the Buddha 's
teachings and meditation.

Timeline Details

2019
Back Home

I began facilitating workshops, meditation programs, and 72 transformations at the studio. Integrating mind and body as one.

Breakthroughs

I knew there was something bigger than what my logical mind could understand. Breakthroughs are the beginning of healing, allowing one to realize they have the power to break free from programming of fear, doubt, stress, depression, the fear of failure and success. Breakthroughs are a part of mastering our awareness. Take the path of uncertainty. The Buddha's teachings show us the path to awakening. Awakening is to observe the depth of our mind.

My journey led me to observe and be aware of what was happening in my life. Frustrations. Unhappiness. I began to feel stuck in this world while having it all; a beautiful loving relationship, falling in love, having two beautiful daughters, a great career, climbing corporate America, owning a home with debts and chasing dreams that I began to realize weren't even mine. These dreams stemmed from programming since I was a child. In 2014, I woke up from this dream, and my reality of uncertainty and fear were gone.

I became the observer of my feelings, emotions, energy and surroundings. For the first time ever, I experienced a feeling of love, compassion and oneness, an experience of enlightenment. What I didn't know at the time was that I needed to heal if I wanted to continue to have that same experience.

Looking back, this was when the warrior mode kick in! I was given a taste and I wanted more! No matter how or where we see our journey beginning or ending, it's the process of it that we are here to observe. Becoming an observer is the true nature and path to understanding oneself.

What should you observe?
Yourself and your own thoughts.
The power is in the question, who am I?

I remember the anxiety and stress I once experienced in my head and having no clue on how to deal with it or why it was there. I was depressed due to my childhood conditions, traumas, and programming. So what was I observing? I started recognizing the fear which kept me from speaking and expressing myself freely without being afraid.

I observed that my thoughts were creating everything. And my emotions (of fear) were connected to these thoughts.

I became excited for this new awareness and the fact that I could choose how to feel in each moment. This was not even close to knowing who I truly am. This was the awakening or the beginning of knowing who I am not. Although many have had this wisdom passed down from ancestors and teachers, it's important to walk your own path to self-discovery. My soul purpose is to help you walk through your own process, and to guide you to discover your true soul's purpose. My guidance is to empower you to break free from the mind of old programming and conditioning.

The warrior within is a journey where you get to experience a change and transformation without spending years of searching. Imagine you become a powerful observer and live a life following your intuition, having the courage to take the step into the unknown and into freedom and liberation.

Transformations

Like I said before, we are all here to observe. For this is the highest level of understanding of the self. No matter what your purpose and impact on the world is, it's your perceptions of what life is and the real you that you will face in your final time here on earth.

Once you get the idea of self-observation, transformation is next. But, transformation cannot take place until you know how to break through the programming that we have been socially engineered and manipulated into accepting. The human trap of suffering. In accepting these beliefs, it may be that you just weren't consciously aware of what's going on around you and the world. The duality of how we perceive to understand through knowledge and learning. It is possible to take your power back but may be frightening if you think you don't know how to do so. No matter how many times we're told to believe that we are all powerful beings, we often still continue to struggle, chasing after the next big thing while trying to pay the bills to survive.

Most of us have programming and imprints on our mind and emotions that create suffering due to not knowing who we truly are or who we think we are. The transformation begins when we take the steps to face what we fear most. This is an expression of our inner truth. I started by taking small steps in breaking all the conditions that I had became aware of at the time. Simple things we can all do, like taking a different route to a routine destination, or stopping at place that we normally don't go to. I decided I did not want to live in fear and full of doubts the rest of my life.

Everyone seemed smarter, more educated, or more successful than I was. Or like they had the perfect family or intimate relationship. Everyone wants to be a superhero, but no one wants to fight the darkness within themselves to get there. To do my best was to surrender to the darkness, remembering I know I am powerful enough to give up everything and trust it will all be okay. I knew I would figure it out. No plans. No answers. But I just wasn't breaking through the programming of my mind.

I also began to notice how my body reacted to fear, love, and joy along with the attachments I had to the material world. I questioned why can some people could create things at will with flow, while others would try to do the same but struggle with it. I came to realize that I didn't need to be concerned with others - it was me that I needed to focus on. I focused on freeing myself from all these emotions of suffering and releasing the need to make everyone happy.

I laughed so hard when I learned the term 'doormat'. And I wondered, "Why the fuck do we as people have labels for everything?" I know it's because of language - that's how we communicate. Yet, at the same time this was something I had struggled with most - language. I started to realize that as a kid, I couldn't get grounded until I learned what grounding meant. Now I can tell you how to ground yourself - from breaking free of the mind all the way to mastering your energy and accessing your power through dream state without needing to know the word grounding. Yes, we are powerful. You just have to believe it and have the courage to trust yourself and break these programs that are running your mind.

Liberations

I want you to know how powerful you are as a human. I want to empower and guide you to discover the power within you, your soul purpose, your remembrance, so you may access the gifts and abilities you may have forgotten about. Your soul waits for you to embark on this warrior journey. Regardless of what we may portray, we are all fighting ourselves as we hide behind titles, labels, education, and so much more. As a warrior, the point of this journey is to remove all these constructs and free ourselves from layers of inner conflict that we have placed upon ourselves for so long in order to survive. We have forgotten that we are powerful, that we are warriors.

The warrior's journey is to bring harmony to the divine feminine and divine masculine and integrate them as one. Transformation is not something to conceptualize, as it is a subjective experience. It can be a lonely path requiring deep solitude and observation. With each breath you breathe you can experience breaking through old patterns and conditions. Creating the transformations.

In this journey, I have learned that it is not what I have or own that makes me strong. It is the awareness and mastering the energy of my own mind and body that brings me strength and liberation. Remembering how to access my powerful warrior light. The light we each breathe in during this temporary human experience.

Liberation...
The journey is never ending.
It can truly begin when you no longer want to carry the heavy armor (what I call life) weighing you down.
...*Life should be free and filled with joy.*

The way you navigate your being is the way you remember who you truly are. You owe it to yourself to take the first step. You are basically a time traveler in this fancy vehicle of human flesh. Now that I have shared a little about myself, it is time to explore each other on a soul-to-soul level, expanding our vibrations closer to the vibration of love one day at a time.

Our time in this human body here on earth is unpredictable. So don't take it for granted and live without regrets!

Although many times these transformations are subtle, they could be the greatest shift of your life. Going into your dreams to observe your subconscious mind to bring your conditioning into the light. It's a dark path that many refuse or fear to face. It is completely liberating when you experience your inner power, tapping into a constant peace, freeing the mind of continuous inner chatter.

My soul purpose is to help people reclaim their inner peace of mind. There are no tools, methods, or instructions needed. Just a simple conversation where we dive deeper into understanding the self.

We explore meditation practices of recognizing that we are not our thoughts and emotions. We are both dark and light. The quicker we face that while we are alive, the more we will be able to shift ourselves from living in this programming state of sleep to the awakened state of awareness. In this state of awareness, we can walk with confidence as we continue to expand our light, while having empathy, love, and compassion for all of life and nature.

The Powerful Questions

Below, are some questions that have helped me during my journey over the past years. I share these with you with the intent to help you jumpstart your thinking process to become more of aware of how your mind is conditioned to think, This is important since your thought process is what creates the routine cycles and habits - things which we may or may not be aware of.

These questions have led me to some of my most powerful thinking, yet have also kept me from overthinking or living in the past or future. To this day they have helped keep me grounded in the present.

We are always in our past and future &
the present is always changing.

These questions are for you! They are simply to get you thinking about your own thoughts. There is no judgment and no right or wrong answers to these questions. And your answers do not define you. Your answers are for you to ponder on and prompt you to think deeper as you continue to shift and expand.

The single most important question...the big WHY...

There's a reason you're reading this book. I'm assuming it's because of something you're wanting to change, there's a deeper suffering you're trying to understand and break free from. First question, whatever that reason is, stop and ask yourself these questions. Find the root of the answer, not generic surface level answer.

- **Why do you continue to suffer?**

_____

_____

_____

_____

_____

_____

_____

_____

_____

_____

Time is an illusion...

How much time do you really have? These questions will keep you grounded and help you to start thinking in the now - with no regrets and knowing there's not limitations.

- **What if you had twenty four hours to live, what would you do?**

- **What if you had ONE WEEK to live, what would you do?**

_____

_____

_____

_____

_____

_____

_____

_____

_____

_____

_____

_____

_____

_____

_____

_____

_____

- **What if you had ONE MONTH to live, what would you do?**

_____

_____

_____

_____

_____

_____

_____

_____

_____

_____

_____

_____

_____

_____

_____

_____

_____

- **What if you had ONE YEAR to live, what would you do?**

_____

_____

_____

_____

_____

_____

_____

_____

_____

_____

_____

_____

_____

_____

_____

_____

_____

_____

- **Knowing there's no tomorrow, who would you become today?**

_____

_____

_____

_____

_____

_____

_____

_____

_____

_____

_____

_____

_____

_____

_____

_____

_____

_____

_____

- **Knowing your past does not define you, who would you become today?**

_____

_____

_____

_____

_____

_____

_____

_____

_____

_____

_____

_____

_____

_____

_____

_____

_____

- **Knowing you only have the present, who are you?**

_____

_____

_____

_____

_____

_____

_____

_____

_____

_____

_____

_____

_____

_____

_____

_____

_____

How has your PAST defined you?

There are people from your past. Some of whom you have not seen in a while. The negative and positive emotions you have about them are part of your warrior journey. You must take responsibility and face the hardest part since we may be in a state of darkness ourselves. Viewing ourselves through the lenses of the past.

- **What specific inner belief systems did you pick up that defined who you were in the past?**

_____

_____

_____

_____

_____

_____

_____

_____

_____

_____

_____

_____

_____

_____

- **In your own mind, how do you think others from your past have defined you or do define you?**

_____

_____

_____

_____

_____

_____

_____

_____

_____

_____

_____

_____

_____

_____

_____

_____

_____

- **In your own mind, how do you think people would see you now or today?**

_____

_____

_____

_____

_____

_____

_____

_____

_____

_____

_____

_____

_____

_____

_____

_____

_____

_____

What defines who you are in the NOW?

These imprints in ourselves create people that come and go in our life. It takes courage and bravery to choose new people, while letting go of the old in order to end conflict and create order of the mind. Your thoughts create the all. You are the creator.

- **How do people define you? The people you surround yourself with...the people in your now.**

_____

_____

_____

_____

_____

_____

_____

_____

_____

_____

- **Why do you surround yourself with these people?**

_____

_____

_____

_____

_____

_____

_____

_____

_____

_____

_____

_____

_____

_____

_____

_____

_____

_____

- **Are you really happy with the people you surround yourself with or is it a way to get away from being alone?** Later we can dive more deeply into why certain people are in your life.

_____

_____

_____

_____

_____

_____

_____

_____

_____

_____

_____

_____

_____

_____

_____

_____

What defines who you are in the FUTURE?

This is where you don't give a fuck about how people define you. How YOU define you in the FUTURE is liberating. It's about becoming all that you are and what you want to be.

Be creative. - Be powerful.
The possibilities are infinite.

_____

_____

_____

_____

_____

_____

_____

_____

_____

_____

_____

You're an infinite being of light!

Healing one moment, one emotion, one word at a time. Sitting in meditation, where you connect your thoughts and emotions without any expectations. Sitting in the present and allowing the flow of your thoughts to surface, allowing them to do their own thing. Just observe what happens and be aware of it.

Suddenly, in a moment, you may feel clarity and wisdom. Sit a little longer. This is mastering awareness (energy). Our thoughts are conditioned (conscious & unconscious programming) based on our individual life experiences thus far. And we have emotions attached to the story behind these thoughts. This is where you vibrate your reality (feelings), analyzing your past and future from an old love story that has been conditioned from childhood traumas and outdated belief systems. Meditation helps with understanding and allowing the flow of what's happening from moment to moment.

We will talk more about integration with meditation more in transformation and liberation.

Decoding vs Unlearning

What I have been experiencing is what many are experiencing collectively: a spiritual awakening. The truth is hidden within us, within the unconscious part of ourselves where we have learned and unlearned from the programming and conditioning. I realize I cannot really unlearn as there is no such thing as unlearning. Once you become aware of something consciously, you are part of it. You begin to have a different perception around what you have learned in the past.

We can reprogram and decode old constructs in the mind without going against your beliefs. Your belief is always your belief, no one can ever change it for you. You may question, though, whether you are fully living in your beliefs. If reading this makes you question your own belief system, perhaps it isn't your truth to begin with. You are not changing it but simply evolving from it by bringing truth into the light. This requires deep meditation. I recently shifted how I expressed things, for it helps you understand something that is beyond words. To simplify, I began expressing my inner truth in a way that is truthful to me.

Let's begin by talking about decoding and reprogramming the mind.

Let's break it into three segments; religion, spirituality, science. Imagine religion was one of the first things you were programmed into believing. You would have developed a core belief from this and lived your life by it. Spirituality is being free from everything that isn't working for you (your programming), which, in this case, is religion. You begin to question everything you have learned by seeking facts, which is science. When you bring all these together in your mind, I call it a technology.

This is why you may become spiritual in the first place. Through the process of how I teach meditation, you'll be able to discover and unveil your own ancient wisdom, knowledge and technology - your natural truth. This is your truth - not thoughts based on things that were taught to you. While seeking this truth and navigating everyday life, you may grind and struggle with your sanity. Eastern religion may refer to this as suffering. You will begin awakening through this suffering process.

We are complicated super human machines with all these thoughts and emotions and the power to decode and reprogram them. As you uncover and reveal these 'new' truths, truths that have been buried for years, there will be a need for a new framework to help you understand them.

Although these new truths may have revealed themselves to you in your past, through, what is called intuition, they may still seem unfamiliar to you if you haven't been listening to your intuition. Trusting your intuition is to follow a calling that we may think is unfamiliar but is actually our real knowing - something the mind cannot comprehend or understand.

Before we get into the framework, I must share what is behind this journey, so I may lead you into your own. We may all have different lives, dreams, and purposes but we are all here to embrace freedom and to live a life full of joy, wealth, and abundance wherever we want to be. The framework involves mapping your own love story timeline, which will help you look deeper into your major life events.

These are the patterns and conditions I have been referring to when we do meditation: bringing the unconscious into your conscious awareness. They say it is dangerous to bring our childhood trauma all up at once, yet the inner warrior has the ability to move through this fearlessly.

We are the only species that delays and suppresses our emotions when we face danger. This is what causes us to live in the past, and hold onto old memories, preventing us from bringing our future into the present.

You may struggle with both your past and future. And you may are not align with your present. This all leads to the frequency not being in full alignment. The framework will help you navigate and integrate as you continue your healing journey using meditation and ancient technology to tune into your crystallized frequency.

From there, we can come back to the body and decode and reprogram your biology (body).

Over the years, I have observed that three conscious living spirits must align; the mind, body, and spirit. I have seen people master one or both, but not all three. Few people I've seen master all three, and the ones that did, are teachers and ancestors who are not around anymore. They left their teachings and energy to help guide us. We live in a different timeline now with information and technology in front of us the majority of the time. It is important to meditate to raise our own technology imprint: our frequency of mind, body and spirit.

Old Program vs Framework

We follow our dreams thinking it is our purpose until we start meditating and observe that some of these dreams are from conditioning and programming. We can start reframing and rewriting our program as we learn to observe. And with these observation changes and integration we start to reframe our life. Our purpose has always been within us. You don't have to search hard for it. When you peel off the layers of old patterns and conditioning, you begin to realize you have actually already been living your purpose.

The framework I refer to is a reference for you to map out your love story – the timeline of major events in your life. There is no rush, be in the present and observe your thoughts of the past and future. We hear a lot about being present which is more difficult than you think. The breath can help you with this and is actually a good test to know whether you are being present. The inhale and exhale are your present. Meditation can help you stay in the present longer as it helps you to become the observer, expanding your awareness.

The framework requires you to investigate your past. Your present is created by your past, so you must go back and observe your past to see how you can reframe your future (by being) in the present. Once you figure out what's been happening to you, you understand what is happening within you. Then, you can break free from these old constructs that are not you.

We are learning to expand this framework so we can see different angles of the same thing, patterns that you have been consciously and unconsciously doing all your life. Remember that you do not need all these labels and information, it is simply guidance to peel back the layers. The information will find you and guide you as needed, while you continue this work through meditation and your healing journey.

Perhaps, you may experience meditation with dragons, spirit guides, masters, and quantum. I am not judging your experience. I have learned over the years, that it is all part of learning and growth. As we continue to observe, we as human beings love to add layers to continue getting away with the old.

The ancients have all these answers, we do not need to keep adding new things! However, we can use new information to effectively communicate with others.

Your meditation will help you drop all of these labels. But, if it does guide you to use such labels, then use them and integrate them to see if it can help you get to where you need to be.

Let's get to the framework. The framework is a routine that you have to dedicate yourself to. The framework I share below is to help guide you on creating your own framework.

Meditation, my most powerful tool, is what the framework is created around. It is important to create time to meditate in the morning and in the evening. It will help you to learn to meditate and become peaceful even when you are in your most stressful moments. We can experience the most powerful transformation when facing our darkest thoughts and emotions. In the chapter Condition vs. Root, I will share more in depth of what these meditations may look like.

The basic framework

Meditation - Body Movement - Breath Work - Nature

Meditation: Over the past 7 years I've routinely started my day with 15-60 minutes of meditation. I've learned that 15 minutes is enough time for me to clear any energy or programming of the mind. I love to sit in meditation and it helps me to teach it as well. I have meditated with groups who have spent over 108,000 + hours meditating (magical numbers) over the years.

Body Movement: I also practice Kung Fu which is a transformation of body movement. I practice my forms then do body movement that helps me release while creating flexibility and free movement. The mind and body will thank you for this as they are deeply connected to one another. This has become a daily ritual, a way of life to feed the mind and body first thing in the morning, and before going to bed.

Breath Work: Breath work is also part of my routine. It's part of the basic framework. Slowly, you will begin to shift and expand. Before you know it, this will ground you into the rest of everything you do in life.

Feeling great and excited? Yes, that is the positive mindset! The creative energy! I can hear you ponder though, "It sounds great, but does it work?" I know life can bring challenges and obstacles, but it's important to make meditation a priority since it will help you reflect on deep issues rooted within. Sometimes we don't want to face these issues because you might think you're creating a "bad" situation or circumstance. I promise you that meditation will give you a new perspective and help you see the world in a more positive light. This framework will give you the ability to respond to and navigate the programming that some call the Matrix, with inner peace.

The programming is not you. The true you is whole and complete, and connected to Mind, Body and Spirit. You can bring in your spirit, ancestors, God, and Source to feel comfortable. They are all invisible forces that will always be with you. Still, there is only YOU in there, in your mind and body. You must take the time to discover what is really you. I believe many people still do not know who they are. Can you be YOU without anything that defines you?

This framework will begin to map your happiest and most joyous moments. Meditation and exercise do not always feel good when you are doing it. We know when we feel good we look good. Start from there. Be gentle to yourself, it can be tough doing it alone. Practice with a group, friends, or someone who can hold you accountable and get you off your feet.

Condition vs Root

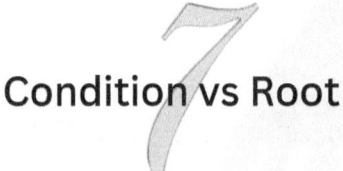

Conditions, conditions and more conditions.
Would you like shampoo with that?

If you start your new framework with daily meditation,
you will become aware of everything in your life that
stems from conditioning. We are talking about getting
to the essence of you, the REAL version of you that has
always been there.

How deep **ARE** your thoughts?

Meditation will expand your awareness to a state of
nothingness. As you meditate, you will go deep into
these old conditions and patterns to explore and
become aware of the programming and conditioning.
No matter how much knowledge we gain, we can still be
conditioned by what we learn.

So, what is it that's really us? Is everything I learned and
everything I've expressed with words part of the
conditioning of such worldly programs?

There is a stillness, an empty void that is calming, peaceful, and quiet. No word can describe the feelings and thoughts that meditation gives me. I am not trying to sell you anything. And I am going to be honest, once you start doing this work it can be really painful to do this work.

We try to use positive vibes to stuff and bury these conditions deeper than we can imagine. But you actually have to free these conditions to reach the true nature of who you are.

That feeling of knowing your own true nature is something that can never be described in words. But you will know it when we are in it. There is nothing to achieve, nothing to accept, and nothing to let go of. It is a simple state of being. This is the "present" that many talk about, but so few actually walk in this nature.

If these conditions are everything that we are, what is bad about accumulating all these things? What about our family, loved ones, our home? I am not saying how you choose to live is a good or bad condition.

If you have achieved and accumulated all these great things and you still feel a sense of not knowing who you are, then you are experiencing some form of conditioning from these programs. If you have achieved and accumulated all these great things, and are completely calm, at ease and peaceful, then great for you!

So, what does it mean to be Rooted? Rooted, in Kung Fu, is a strong foundation of our body structure, while moving and standing still. Like the root of a tree. The degree to which a tree can withstand the winds and storms is all dependent on the strength of its roots. If it is rooted well, it will have a strong foundation. If it is not rooted well, it will easily be taken down by adverse weather.

Your mind, body and spirit are the roots to your very essence. Although we often think the mind is rooted in the brain, the mind itself actually does not have roots. Just like the spirit, it is not physical. In one of my workshops, I teach the simple emptiness meditation. This meditation guides us to understand the true essence of our mind.

Pause for one minute, close your eyes and visualize yourself reaching out to everything you know. Starting with yourself, reach out to all of your situations, experiences, achievements, and loved ones. It may seem that you cannot touch it as it cannot be reached. Yet you may feel a sensation that is the root.

The real root of you has no labels.

We are not here to find enlightenment, even though it is possible. We are here to observe the conditions that are creating this duality and endless conflicts. We do this because breaking through this we know who we truly are.

Self-Mastery vs Self-Mystery

We need to walk through the mystery of self before experiencing self-mastery. But what direction should we take? It seems like the conditioning is never ending as we continue to seek direction from others while we walk our own journey. Sometimes we walk through our own misery before we can walk and embody self-mastery and discovery.

Life is simple and it has become simple for me since I became aware of everything. Once you get out of these cycles and take time to breathe, you begin remembering who you are. This is self-mastery and self-realization.

While being in the moment, one can recognize that self-pity and mystery are dark clouds creating emotional conflict. Even though surrendering and letting go of this emotional conflict may be for the highest good, we find ourselves hanging on to these things with hope.

Sitting in meditation is where I find breakthroughs, and where I am able to free the mind of programming.

Mystery is difficult for us to navigate in this life because we try to exercise too much control. We try to force our way through life by trying to make things happen and not knowing how to release these patterns.

The conditioning has been embedded in our subconscious for far too long and we end up speaking about doing things which we don't really even intend to do because of such conditioning. We do it to please others hoping they will love us in return.

Once we are able to recognize this mystery, the unknown, and realize it as part of our growth, we can be still and observe the dark clouds as they eventually pass and transform into clear blue clouds and rainbows.

To embrace self-mastery is to transform these experiences into inner knowing and wisdom. This requires you to pay full attention to your thoughts and awareness and be in a state of full observation. This will allow you to respond with inner peace and eventually leads to the self-mastery. It takes time and mindfulness to untangle the conditions of your thoughts that have become habitual.

Transformation can only happen when we start to face our fears and trust our intuition. Taking small steps to remove the fear of lack, self-doubt, shame, embarrassment, along with the fear of failure to success. All these feelings and emotions stem from our conditioning. It takes courage to break through and overcome these feelings of fear and shame and doubt.

One of the simplest things I teach is to observe your daily habits and routine. In the beginning, fear will arise so start small. Take small baby steps to confront your thoughts. Pay attention to what your mind tells you to do, and how your heart (emotions) may feel something else. The more you meditate and practice, the closer you get to that state of self-mastery.

Personally, it has taken me over 7 years of facing and breaking down my own old conditioning and programming to get to self-mastery. Now, I operate my life in awareness around my conscious and subconscious mind. I operate with knowing my boundaries, attachments, detachments, desires, wants, and creations.

I am willing and able to take the path less traveled, away from the mainstream and allowing everything that needs to show up on my journey to show up. I may not have the answers, but I do know I am supported as I take steps closer to self-mastery. I trust, because I know we live in an abundant universe.

I embrace the path of uncertainty and the unknown. I know the path I was on comes from the linear thought process, which merely comes from my past experiences and knowledge.

If I wish to open the doorway to receive what God or the Universe intends for me to receive, I must have trust. There will be fear walking through this doorway, stepping into the unknown with no security, but it is beyond anyone's understanding. It is for me to face and master my own experience and wisdom.

You will not find instructions or methods in this reading. You will find symbols from the experiences I share, that may or may not resonate with you. This will help you find what is already within you. Self-mastery takes years, perhaps a lifetime to master.

Once you embrace who you truly are, your life will operate on a new level. You will set your own boundaries, share your wants, speak authentically, and decide what to respond to and how to respond. No means no! You'll begin to read others very well by reading and knowing yourself. You'll question things and exploring the answers to these questions will be your next breakthrough. It will not concern you what others think. You'll be aware your inner thoughts and conflicts from the old programming.

What you adapted to and learned from the world around you, you took as truth and fact. You accepted things as the truth because you were surrounded by people who also felt the same way. Self-mastery requires understanding and integrating both the darkness and the light. It's unavoidable but will get easier as you meditate. The thoughts can stop as it is just energy, trapped energy that is built up from emotion. Sometimes this holding onto things makes it hard to express who you truly are. I will expand more on self- expression and expansion later.

Meditation has become one of my most trusted tools and routines. You can sit quietly to pray, or to relax and reset. The longer you sit, the more space you create for the mind to expand. This new space is clear, quiet, and still. It gives you control and power, allowing you to reprogram your mind, transforming reaction into awareness and responding. Your ability to focus and be in the present requires your full attention to these thoughts.

My meditation has allowed me to step back and see all that is happening in my life. The practice will become a part of you as you learn to become the observer and act and respond in alignment with your soul purpose.

Yes, we make mistakes but there are no accidents. It's not a mistake when we feel our decision is the right one at that moment. You will learn not to dwell on your past, as this too is part of your self-mystery to self-mastery.

Darkness vs Light

Fear comes to mind when we speak about darkness versus light. We are always looking to bring in more light. Sometimes many people walk around in darkness their entire life. This is due to programming and not being able to self-reflect or observe what is happening.

But, we don't see it as programming because it's become so engrained as our core belief. This belief keeps us in the dark, while we seek the light outside, waiting for someone to turn it on. We have to turn the light on ourselves, it is always present. Darkness is a collective consciousness construct that we are learning to navigate while co-existing in this world.

Fear comes in so many different forms, and I refer to it as a state of mind from programming, belief systems, negative emotions, entities, images, and imaginations. It is an entity created by our own collective illusion that we all experience energetically. It is a state of illusion from our imagination. The darkness is showing up in our lives as a teacher. We must learn about the darkness as something that is part of us,

Something we carry unconsciously which has to be brought to the light in order to expand. Our darkness shows us where light is needed. We may then embrace it and see through it. So how is it some people walk easier through life and rarely encounter darkness, while others can be compassionate and loving but seem to always be dealing with darkness in their reality?

Many say we are here for the human experience and to do our best and just have trust and faith. These are all good, but do we really know what we are doing, or are we blindly trusting what others are saying without questioning it? Does your belief system work for you?

The human experience is a gentle way of saying it is okay if you mess up. Making mistakes is part of the process and healing. The human experience is part of self-mastery and self-realization. Truth is ever present, but everyone's truth is unique to them. You must uncover and remember your very own truth. Liberation is being free from fear and darkness. I don't mention much about light, as you do not need to be reminded of light, for that is what you are.

Experiencing light looks like when you are having fun in life, laughing, playing and creating. With the light, you begin mastering your darkness and see through programs and conditions that keep you stuck in negative patterns.

Trauma and conditioning block us from seeing who we truly are. Even if we have no idea about these traumas or conditions, we try to bypass it by projecting these out into the world. We seek help of others who have been through similar experiences, even though the experiences are never quite the same. We are individual, and we can only walk our own journey.

Support groups, mentors and coaching can guide us through this journey, but it is up to you to do your work. Transformation is not measured by success or anything of material nature. Transformation is inner work, self-reflection and liberation from suffering that we created by our very own unconscious and conscious illusion.

Not everything is a choice, we are conditioned by choices that we think we are choosing but that is not always the case.

Freedom vs Illusion of Choice

It seems our thinking stems from our programming. We feel empowered by our ability to choose. But is there actually freedom of choice or is it just the illusion of choice? There is a difference in making a choice based on our conditioning vs. using our intuition, our inner knowing.

Often, we do not know what we want. We dream or think of some form or idea in our mind. Some of these ideas come from our true authentic self, while others come from our conditioning from society and others' opinions. When the mind is clear of clutter, doubt, fear and expectation, we walk in our true state of being, without these titles and labels that create an illusion of the self. We are still very individual. The knowing of oneness and experience of self will be another topic which I will bring awareness to later.

Most choices stem from a false sense of security and conditioning. Freedom is when we embody and free ourselves from expectations and embrace uncertainty, realizing there is no such thing as security.

But what are we supposed to do when conflict arises when we make a decision?

The answer is to be at peace with whatever the outcome is. This is much easier said than done but this is exactly why meditation is such a powerful tool. Challenges arise constantly. Yet, nowadays I am able to sit for 15 minutes to shift my conflicts, bringing clarity allowing me to make the right decision. It's not the choice that gives me the freedom, but the clarity that I have no expectation of the outcome. The decision I make is from the heart and in the moment. Some thinking and analyzing may come into play, but there is no manipulation or giving away my energy which would create further conflict. When you know who you are, you operate with integrity.

Looking back at my life, I have found that many of my best decisions were my choice. It was a push coming from my own anger and fear to take a jump into the unknown and uncertainty. It is how I discovered living in the present is not as easy as I write about.

How can we tell people to live in the present, when we tell them to create their future at the same time? Isn't this contradictory to what the present is? There is nothing here that is right or wrong.

If we continue to think that having a choice is freedom yet there is still an underlying conflict, we will continue to suffer. Our decision making has been conditioned from a very young age by how our parents raised us. This holds true, even for simple things like choosing an ice-cream. As an adult we start to realize, it was all an illusion of choice.

Why can't we choose ice-cream without any form of manipulation? Understanding this gives us the freedom that no matter what decision we take, we suffer less when we are okay with any outcome, having no expectations. This may not be new information to you.

The challenging part of life is that we may be in situations where we are caught up in the drama and situations, entangled with other people. We may be afraid to step into our own power, worrying about hurting other people if we share our authentic self and what we really want.

Instead, we suffer and hurt ourselves by pushing our choices to the side instead of having a compassionate, loving conversation with one another and allowing each other to have a different opinion and belief.

Society taught us that if we don't get what we want, we can force others to comply due to legal matters of the law. Man-made laws are BS. The natural law of nature that governs us should be the highest law of love and kindness as this is the truth and integrity.

Expression Without Expansion

You do not need a choice when you know the "I", your individuality. Let's expand on the "I", the self that is here to experience this human emotional roller coaster. Unaware that you have been programmed since birth. You are here to express your individuality no matter what belief you have cultivated around oneness or enlightenment. Do not fall into the BS of oneness when you are not aware of who you are.

We have this conditioning that we should be caring and loving to everyone even if we're suffering in our own misery. Until we understand what the "me" and "I" stand for, we are unable to authentically share this. The fact that you cannot sleep without anxiety and stress, is why you are living in someone else's head.

Meditation has taught me that the root of all my problems come from fitting into the box of everyone else's ideals. I stay in a container for them to feel comfortable around me, pleasing them by complying to their reality. This is not about being negative or positive.

It is the simplest thing that we may see each other as different people, but do we really allow one other to express our truths and listen to them? The "I" is also the "we" as we wish to see a better world by moving into "oneness" and embracing this we-ness and weird-ness.

You live in a state of rationalization, everything you choose is based on rationalization. Instead of allowing your being to express itself, you suffer. The "I" must express itself and expand. What are we expanding? Are you expanding, or are you projecting? Having the ability to memorize a quote and repeat things is not truly expanding, it is projecting and wanting. A desire to become something we really are not, so we adapt to please and fit into society.

What defines the "I" is how you define yourself. You are here to experience the release of the illusion of the Self; to stop the Self from defining itself. Realization is a self-discovery journey, and it is why you are here to write your own love story.

It is the simplest thing that we may see each other as different people. But do we really allow each other to express our truths and listen to them?

To be a different person, different than our own expectations?

This is all ancient knowledge and we keep getting further away from it. When in fact we actually have a basic level of need for this knowledge. We have not uncovered these truths that are buried deep within our minds. We continue to buy into the notion of more is better, or less is better.

There is freedom of the self, cultivating the "I", knowing we are one, and ignoring this "I" exists for a reason. Understanding knowledge alone does not free us. Understanding and wisdom comes from living and being (present) while doing so. We can experience all that life has to offer us. We also have the opportunity to know where conflicts come from and how our self-expression and expansion will free us from all programs, war, hate, security, and attachments.

Suddenly, you awaken. But not awakening as the mainstream discusses with all its labels. Awaken, where we realize these labels give us conflict around who we truly are, the "I", "me", self and oneness of our very existence.

Intuition vs Super Intuition

Now let's dive into the super intuition journey together, are you ready? We have learned that intuition is one of the most important things to recognize within us. There have been many times that my intuition has guided me on the right path of uncertainty and the unknown, while my logical mind could never understand it. There was no answer, no matter how hard I tried to rationalize why I would choose something or not.

Intuition can be scary though. The signs are present, but not always clear in the moment. You have to trust your gut feelings that speak in silent tones of the unknown path. Sometimes when we follow the inner calling of our intuition, there is no turning back. It can lead us to danger if we do not pay attention to it, or it can lead us to opportunities that open doors to brand new things.

Meditation of 7 years has opened up this superpower of intuition for me and it only continues to grow stronger. I trust my intuition and my gut instincts before the thoughts start to seep in.

By trusting my intuition, I stop all conflict by not allowing it to reach the logical thinking mind. My intention is to trust my first intuitive calling, along with my past experiences and knowledge, to prepare me for my journey. If conflict arises in the thought process, then I sit still and feel the emotions. I do not sit still to have clarity. I sit still to clear the energies of the thoughts and feelings, allowing my intuition to sharpen.

When do I not trust my intuition? Has my intuition led me to failure or on the wrong path? Perhaps it is not failure, but rather misinterpretation of my intuition. That is why it is important to pay attention to your shadow side and blind spots, and do the shadow work. When we are not aware of what our blind spots are that stem from traumas and conditioning, our intuition will be misinterpreted by both our emotions and our mind.

We can only truly understand from understanding our own fears . Take synchronicities for example. Every synchronicity in life is a gem that life drops on us that, if we pay attention, we can pick up as clues. These same jewels and gems have often led me to follow unhealed wounds and conflicts from my past that I might have been able to avoid if I had these tools growing up.

The journey of self-discovery and remembering how to navigate my inner awareness has given me the ability to share these tools with you. There is no accident, luck or miracle. It is not because I do or do not believe in them, but because it blinds me from seeing my true-self, gifts and power.

You have these same power, gifts, awareness, inner knowledge and wisdom to guide you through life with very little external influences. When you see gems and synchronicities, you can navigate where you want to head with freedom of choice from your soul. You are free to choose without conditioning or conflict.

Are you ready for your own love story? I feel that your love story is important in order to discover, remember and come home to yourself. I am able to write this today because I have healed through my own trauma, conditioning and programming of the mind. I know we have this ability to remember our power, love, joy, and peace. This is our nature and birthright, our liberation and freedom. Lastly, what defines you and what you define as yourself isn't really you in the first place. You are love, you are powerful, you are sovereignty!

Ritual and Routine

Personally, I am not a big fan of routines and rituals, because -for me- it stops the free flow of simply being. I understand that it is important to have them in order to integrate what I have learned and discovered. It's also helpful in supporting the mind, body and soul.

I have shared my daily routines, and intermittent practices that if I miss them in my life, I can always go back to. Humans are creatures of habit, although I like to break old habits. There is comfort in some of our habits, but addictions can keep us from living and following the heart.

Meditation- It is a tool, the only powerful ancient technology that allows me to master energy, inner awareness, expansion and breaking free from old programming. It allows me to heal from within and change my external reality. I practice meditation when I wake up, in the middle of the day and night, at least three times a day to reset and clear my thoughts.

Kung Fu - Kung Fu is my life. Before meditation, Kung Fu helped me understand my body, by creating confidence, and improving body movement, strength and flexibility. I practice Kung Fu three or four times a week, including when I teach Kung Fu wellness for kids and adults. It keeps my mind and body focused and relaxed and gives me the ability to respond with fluidity and gentleness. There are misconceptions around Kung Fu and Martial Arts being termed where it is considered a hard core fighting sport. However, Kung Fu is not meant as a hard core fighting sport and not everyone that practices has the skillset to be a fighter or master the skillset. Yet, Kung Fu gives another layer of self-mastery of one mind and body connection. The more you practice, the more gentle and relaxed you feel while developing inner strength.

Sleep & Dream - There is a whole other level of sleep and dream state. This helped me learn and navigate through my journey. Dreams are parallel to our waking reality, and there is another universe you get to master as you master your own energy. Sleep is so important. It is important to recharge, rest and reset and sleeping allows for you to do this.

Nature - Lastly, get as much sunlight, water, and nature as possible. As I integrated these, I became more aware of all my fears, doubts and conditions. It helped me to break free from habits and thoughts that controlled me. It's not about control, it is about knowing the true you without all the illusions. It takes courage to discover and continue your awakening journey, walking away from things that keep you suffering. Only you can discover what these are. Having a mentor, coach, teacher or professional that walk their talk can help you one step closer to your liberation. I am grateful for all that has been in my life, past, present and future.

I am who I am today because you are here to show me something about myself. I love to show you and guide you through this journey to empower you, and help you remember you have had this power all along. Reach out and I would love to hear your love story. You matter, you are enough, and you are always loved!

DEDICATIONS
With love & Gratitude

My Powerful Daughters

This is dedicated to my daughters Abbie Huynh and Ava Huynh. To my beautiful and powerful girls! Someday I know my work can be a light that casts out any shadow or challenge you may have in your journey. Dad wants to leave this record of my journey and legacy for both of you. I know that this tool can guide you back to your own self-love and self-discovery journey. No matter how challenging life may be, I choose to take the hardest path, that is to pave this new energy and road for both of you to walk more in your love, light and sovereignty. Now matter when the time is, if you are reading it today, tomorrow or someday in the future, know that my love for you is always there. Knowing that your father is a powerful being, so are you and don't ever forget that. Being powerful with love, compassion and wisdom, you get to choose how you want to live. So you do not have to be afraid of anyone or anything. This illusion of life will pass by so fast, all you will have are memories that will eventually fade away as the days pass. Live to your fullest, happiest and most joyful moments every day. I always love you both, you're always loved - Papa

His Eminence Shyalpa Tenzin Rinpoche

I first heard of Rinpoche in Clubhouse, an audio-based social media app that allows people everywhere to talk, tell stories, develop ideas, collaborate and meet new people all around the world. I would hop into his "room(s)" to listen and raise my hand wanting to introduce myself and share my experiences and wisdom in the same space as his Eminence. He would always bring me up to speak when I raised my hand but I never really spoke with him. I would either drop out or leave the room before it was my turn.

I thought Rinpoche seemed to be pretty cool to be talking and teaching on a public forum like Clubhouse. I have never seen any other Rinpoche in clubhouse apps, and I know many teachers are busy with their teaching at their monastery.

I had sent Rinpoche a few back channel messages in Clubhouse and he actually responded. I was so impressed and appreciative of how real and down to earth he was.

Typically in most places, it is very hard to get in contact with a Rinpoche because they are so busy with their practice and ritual. When I decided to write this book, I thought it would be so cool if Rinpoche would write a foreword and a review for my book. So I emailed him and asked him for his blessing and I got a response: "YES, SEND IT TO ME". This teaches me how compassionate and open he is. As busy as his Holiness is, he still took the time to support me and write a forward for my book. I have so much to learn from him and his teaching of love and compassion. Rinpoche is a true enlightened being here to teach us to cultivate love, wisdom and compassion. Please help in sharing my gratitude to Rinpoche by supporting his vision: https://www.peacesanctuary.org/ https://www.buddhafield.us/shyalpa-rinpoche

"You follow a genuine spiritual lineage by striving to be the best that you can be. My teachers have always done their best to realize their own pure essence. These great masters are never corrupted by desire for personal gain or glory. This is the virtue of a lineage that is golden and untarnished."

~ Shyalpa Tenzin Rinpoche

Caitlin Leigh Fluegge

Caitlin and I connected through Simbi exchange in Sep 2021. She has an amazing and interesting full-time business of dog sitting. I was so interested in what she does as dog sitting, I invited her to my first podcast in December 2021. You can listen to her passionately talk about her business in that podcast here: https://anchor.fm/imchoying/episodes/ESP-49-The-Goddess-of-Doggie-Sitter-e1bcnla).

Because she's had experience with publishing her own poetry books, she was the first person I reached out to help edit this book. She is so energetically loving and full of light and laughter. I want to give her the gratitude for crossing paths and being in my life. Caitlin is an author of several books of poetry (which aligns very closely with my philosophy), an artist, dog sitter, Reiki Master & Graced Practitioner. She has a Master's degree in Transpersonal Psychology with an emphasis in Ecopsychology and Life Coaching, along with several certifications in energy healing.

Please help in sharing my gratitude to Caitlin by supporting her here: https://linktr.ee/caitlinleigh777

Yannae Kemp

Yannae Kemp, my soul brother, I met Yannae while collaborating together for a retreat. Every time I hear him speak, he speaks with intention and purpose with his words and carries his being as a loving and powerful man. What I love about Yannae is he speaks gentleness with power and kindness around everything he does. He gives encouragement and empowerment to you no matter who you're. Yannae is one of the many friends I mention where I can totally trust my life with. Recently I saw Yannae sharing a video talking about his experience of the 369 Manifestation. I had a strong calling to listen to that video. I reached out to Yannae to catch up and told him that since seeing his video, I and a group of friends have also been practicing the 369 method. When I started the 369 Manifestation practice is when this book started flowing through me. I give a lot of gratitude and respect to Yannae. Everything Yannae speaks is intentional and helping youth to cultivate their love and power. Yannae Kemp is a Certified Health and Life Coach, S.E.L Educator, Motivational Speaker. Please help in sharing my gratitude to Yannae by supporting him here at www.ytkservices.com

Yvette Van Dam

When Yvette and I met in 2018 at Kopan Monastery, we were practicing a 90-day Abundance Meditation and were also on the same discussion team and course. She had unique ways with words and a profound wisdom when speaking in our class. She is strong-willed and willing to help you out when needed. While keeping in touch with her after the monastery, I became aware that I still needed healing myself and that I was blocked when trying to speak my thoughts out loud with words. I recalled that when she asked me questions I would try to answer by text but it was taking me too long to answer. So I started leaving her audio message responses. It was then that I discovered I needed to work on getting the thoughts out of my head and into spoken words. Over the years we have continued to communicate and and hold space for each other. Empowering and encouraging each other in our continued dharma practice. She is also an incredibly intuitive healer and reader. Yvette has given so much support to me in editing this book, it couldn't be possible and wouldn't be the same without her. Please help in sharing my gratitude to Yvette by supporting her here at http://byyvette.com/

Shashwat Bhardwaj

Our story starts with me introducing myself to him and addressing him with the wrong name (the same name as a person from another retreat I had attended back in 2016.) Shashwat came to sit down at my table the first dinner night. He is charmic, handsome and intelligent young man. We hit it off as part of my soul brother in the same soul family. Our conversation was fun and energetic as we talked about where he used to work at the Tiger sanctuary in India. We started our friendship with laughter and not taking life seriously. If I recall, we sat together during our lunch and dinner every day at our retreat. We have been friends and also kept connected over the years. Shashwat is one of the people I know, who has read and studied many books in all areas. He has so much wisdom and knowledge of a guru. So much that leads me to believe he is an incarnated as a wise young man, who lived many lifetimes as a guru teacher. It's my honor to have him read this book, which means a lot to me. I want to honor Shashwat as an amazing brother and friendship over the years. He is a private person. If you love to interview or speak to him, let me know. I always suggest that he start sharing his knowledge and wisdom with the world.

Emerald Raye

Emerald is my beloved podcast co-host who's taught me the kindness and compassionate of always believing in myself and others. We met on Clubhouse, sharing similar philosophy and wisdom. Quickly we started hosting rooms on Clubhouse and now we share our experiences together on our pod cast "Inner Transformations". Her wisdom and compassion speaks from a highly energetic level. She sees things that others normally wouldn't and helps them navigate their life challenges emotionally and energetically. She has been coaching clients for years helping them to see things inwardly and to understand of our mindset transformations. Our podcast of sharing wisdom and love wouldn't be possible without her. As an "Energy Strategist " she determines what energetic fields are being used to form ones outer environment. This energy field functions as an attractor or repellent throughout one's life, to restore "CREATIVE CONFIDENCE" thru unifying the Inner Mind's masculine and feminine frequencies. Please support and connect with Emerald Raye at emeraldray777@gmail.com Inner Transformation podcast on Anchor and Spotify: https://anchor.fm/innertransformations

Holly Finnegan

Holly came to my studio back in 2019. At the time I was not teaching the meditations. Instead, a great friend of mine was leading them. For me, meditation was always far more deeper than just sitting and breathing in and out. Looking back, I was waiting for someone who wanted to dive deeper into meditation with dialogues, questions and doing the routine practice of breaking free of these conditions of the mind (which was my intention when I opened the studio). The studio was only open for a few months at the time that Holly started coming so there wasn't many people who were consistently coming. Holly was the one who started to return on a weekly basis and started to ask questions. I eventually began to lead the meditation myself, but always did so based on my intuition for that day. We would sit and meditate either in silence or I'd add some music from time to time for any new students then we would end our meditation with group discussion. Fast forward, 3+ years later, I can say she has been one of the longest students now.

She has become one of my teachers, as we both continue our daily discussion, dialogues and meditation along with shamanic healing work. The gift Holly brings is incredible power and compassion. A powerful voice of expression, a powerful speaker, She has been doing this work for more than 3+ years, not including her own soul work before coming to my studio. No one else I know has the mind that she has with her ability to organize and apply structure and see things far ahead. She discovered that her soul purpose is to create SILO - Spaces Intended for Loving Ourselves. A space for others just like all of us, going through our inner journey and sharing our experience helping others to love ourselves, in a space without judgment regardless of where we come from. We have partnered in hosting workshops, classes, retreats. We are currently working together to create SILO and Inner Chatter which is a concept built upon gathering together for intentional, purposeful conversation and interactive activities to bring positive light and support to all. Holly is powerful, loving and kind. She is willing to give up her time to help anyone. So if you love what she is creating, please support and reach out to Holly.

Joseph Williams

Joseph and I met outside of the coffee shop. He was wearing a shirt with the Chinese character meaning dream. We struck a conversation and I knew there was a depth and knowledge with Joseph's spiritual being. (We now call each other spiritual warriors: iron sharpen iron.) He's attended my meditation workshop and ever since we've been doing soul work together as soul brothers of light. His presence radiates God's shield of light. The amazing thing about Joseph, is he can create anything he desires with his mind and will. His son Kolt has been my Kung Fu student for a year and a half. Joseph sees the importance of meditation and Kung Fu and every week he dedicates over an hour to bring Kolt to class. I cannot wait to see Joseph and Kolt on where they will be in supporting this world as vibrational leaders of divine men. Please help in sharing my gratitude to Joseph and support with love.

Joseph-William exQuisite

Natural Blackberry Wine

Top Regional Brick -n- Mortar Venue

Farmersville Il

618-401-7376

Joseph_William_exQuisite@protonmail.com